Vietnam '66

A Personal Experience
of the War

By Jim Burns

2015

Published by:
    Memini, an imprint of
    Pietas Publications
    Waynesboro, VA U.S.A.
    Phone: 1-540-221-4142
    Email: pietas@jasperburns.com
Printed and bound in the United States of America.

CONTENTS

PREFACE

Since early in their war against the French, Vietnamese forces had been digging tunnels for both strategic and tactical purposes. Only in the mid-1960s did Americans fully realize the extent of these tunnels and the dangers they presented. Most of the tunnels were destroyed by 1969, but not before they had provided concealment and surprise to many communist military operations, including the crucial turning point known as the Tet Offensive.

My experience was that of a civilian scientist studying the geologic settings where tunnels were built. My aims were (1) to predict where tunneling might or might not be feasible, so as to give guidance for search operations; and (2) to determine the soil properties that would have to be considered in the design of tunnel-detection apparatus.

My status as a civilian on a military project gave unusual opportunities to observe and work with American soldiers on the front lines as well as in headquarters, to meet with Vietnamese government officials and, while living in Saigon, to become acquainted with ordinary people to the extent that language allowed.

The experience triggered a gradual transformation in my thoughts about the war, both as I observed it personally and as I learned of its larger context. As the war fades in our national memory, I find it increasingly useful to review my understanding of that larger context.

When Americans speak of the Vietnam War, we refer to a conflict that gained worldwide attention through 21 years, from 1954 to 1975. It was a conflict in which North Vietnam and its Viet Cong allies in South Vietnam opposed the government of South Vietnam and its allies, principally the United States. It is the only war in which most Americans freely admit to having been defeated. It altered our domestic politics and our social fabric in ways that still persist.

In Vietnam, this war is known as the Resistance War against America, or the War against the Americans to Save the Nation, or simply the American War. It is also known as the Second Indochina War. The First Indochina War, known in Vietnam as the Anti-French Resistance War, lasted from 1946 to 1954. After years of stalemate, it ended with the French defeat at Dien Bien Phu.

Vietnam had become a French colony through a process lasting from the middle to the late years of the 19th century. The colony was occupied by Japan during the Second World War.

From these dates we see the longtime context in which the Vietnamese sought independence and unity. There is also a significant political context involving the major powers.

The American War was an integral part of the Cold War. North Vietnam was supported by communist countries including the Soviet Union, China, and North Korea. South Vietnam was supported by anti-communist countries including the United States, Thailand, Australia, New Zealand, and the Philippines.

The American policy of "containing" communist powers – taking steps to prevent their expansion – was in direct conflict with the policy voiced by Soviet Premier Khrushchev when he hailed the development of such "Wars of National Liberation" as the new model for spreading communist doctrine and control, and for overcoming resistance by the capitalistic nations.

Because of its link to the Cold War, the Vietnam War soon became a key element of domestic political considerations in the United States.

Cast of characters and organizations:

The narrative includes frequent mention of the following people and organizations without specific introductions.

Office of the Secretary of Defense/Advance Research Projects Agency (variously abbreviated as OSD/ARPA or ARPA). The gov-

ernment office that sponsored and directed the tunnel research program. Headquartered in Washington, DC. Operated a field office in Saigon.

Research Analysis Corporation (RAC). My employer, a private not-for-profit research organization under contract to ARPA and other defense agencies. Headquartered in McLean, VA. Operated a field office in Saigon.

Other RAC employees included: Perry F. Narten, a geologist from the McLean office who was assigned as my partner in the tunnel project. Dorothy Clark and Harry Handler, professional staff members on long-term assignment in the Saigon field office.

Viet Cong (often referred to as VC or Victor Charlie). A political and military organization in South Vietnam that fought U.S. and South Vietnamese forces. I understand that this was a pejorative term shortened from expressions meaning "Vietnamese Communist" and "Communist Traitor to Vietnam." A preferred term in peacetime is National Liberation Front for South Vietnam. The term VC referred both to the organization and to its individual members. It was distinct from the North Vietnamese troops who also entered the war.

Republic of Vietnam (RVN). The government of South Vietnam during the war. Its army was generally designated by the abbreviation ARVN.

J.R.B.

ACKNOWLEDGMENTS AND DEDICATION

This book is based on a knowledge and understanding of Viet Cong tunnels that could never have been acquired without tireless and courageous efforts by members of the armed forces of the United States and its allies in Vietnam. Some of these are named in the narrative, but names of the vast majority are unknown to me.

Among these are the heroes known admiringly as "tunnel rats" or "tunnel runners," who demonstrated stunning courage as they entered the dark underground world of tunnels and water wells to probe their secrets. They risked ambush, booby traps of advanced as well as primitive design, and the ever-present danger that the ground might collapse upon them.

Also included are those who were diligent and creative in research, intelligence analysis, and the development of training materials for tunnel warfare. Together, they produced a coherent picture of the activity that greatly benefited our fighting forces. They willingly shared their findings with others, including me.

The book is dedicated to those who gave their lives in these efforts.

ABOUT THE AUTHOR

Jim Burns has previously written and published three books:

THE COLD COASTS, A Cold War Caper in the High Arctic. Describing a field assignment in Svalbard.

WORKING CLASS HERO, One Life in a Stalwart Generation 1884-1954. About the life and times of his father.

ONCE UPON A BLOG, Contents of the Blog "Jim's Observations" from August 2013 to September 2014. Recollections, adventures, and opinions from a long and varied life.

The current book originated as a series of blog posts about the Vietnam War, based on the author's assignment there in 1966. The posts were popular both in the United States and abroad. The purpose of this book is to provide a compact printed record of them, without extraneous materials.

I. The Preliminaries

EASTER BUNNY

My first brush with Vietnam took place during the weekend of Easter Sunday, April 18, 1954. At that time, we still spoke of the place as French Indochina. The final major engagement between French and Vietnamese Nationalist forces under Ho Chi Minh, at Dien Bien Phu, was underway. It had been going on for three months and would end on May 7 with defeat for the French. They would soon leave the region.

Good Friday was a slow day at the office. Our family was having an up-and-down year of high pressure thus far. My wife's mother suffered a major stroke in January. Our second child, a son, was born in February. My father died in March. Now, April was bringing a beautiful spring and we were looking forward to a quiet, restful enjoyment of the weekend.

About mid-afternoon, the bosses called us together. We had a "quickie" project on our hands. We needed to produce a terrain study covering most of what we now know as Vietnam. This would consist of several sets of map overlays describing geology, soils, landforms, and water supply and drainage conditions in the region. There would also be overlays addressing military implications such as the ability of tanks and other vehicles to maneuver off roads ("cross-country movement," we called it), and the suitability of the terrain for constructing roads and airfields.

We were members of the Military Geology Branch (MGB), U.S. Geological Survey, and this was one of the kinds of work that we did. Meanwhile, our colleagues at the Army Map Service would be adding studies of existing roads and airfields. In our usual whimsical fashion, we named this project "Easter Bunny." A project like this would normally occupy at least half a dozen people for about two months. We were told on Friday afternoon that we would have to deliver final camera-ready copy by early the next Tuesday morning. Arrangements were made to keep various governmental libraries, map collections, and aerial photo collections open through the weekend, so that they could provide us with the source materials we needed.

Staff members of the Military Geology Branch meeting late at night to plan a "quickie" project.

We put about 30 people to work on the project. Even so, the schedule seemed daunting. It will suffice to say that very few of the 30 managed to go home for a night's sleep between Friday and Tuesday. We made the deadline.

About two weeks later, we were invited to what was called a "debriefing" by a joint military team just returned from Indochina. They proceeded to make clear how our effort had fitted into the machinery of presidential decision-making.

In the waning days of Dien Bien Phu, President Eisenhower had requested a briefing on what actions the United States might be able to take that could influence the outcome of the battle. There is no doubt that he considered many factors beyond our purview, but we were kept informed on the particular role that Easter Bunny had played.

This joint military team had been assembled to examine the situation on the ground, and then to report their findings to the President. This had to be done in a few days. They requested a terrain study, among other things, to direct their attention to the principal problem areas quickly and efficiently. In a sense, they would be field-checking our results and determining their implications for national policy.

The primitive condition of the existing road net and airfields, the widespread terrain conditions that would seriously hamper road and airfield construction, and the difficulty of the terrain for any off-road movement, all led to the following conclusions during the presidential briefing: **At that time, the United States could not provide the logistical support needed for large military units operating in Indochina. We could support only small units the size of one regiment or smaller.**

I have no way of knowing what else the President considered, but the joint military team felt strongly that these conclusions regarding logistical support played heavily into his decision not to enter the fray in Indochina at that time. We took pride in our contribution of Project Easter Bunny.

UNCONVENTIONAL WARFARE

Within the next ten years, research into the "art of war" as practiced in the Vietnam conflict had become a growth industry. We used various terms, such as "unconventional warfare" and "remote area conflict." This research seemed to have a lively future. Nikita Khrushchev spoke of "wars of national liberation," as the new model for Communist expansion, following the indecisive results of conventional warfare in Korea.

In 1964, after serving four years as Assistant Chief of the Military Geology Branch (MGB), I welcomed the opportunity for a one-year assignment with the Army Engineer Waterways Experiment Station (WES) in Vicksburg, Mississippi. WES was involved in research important to the future of military geology, studying new applications to unconventional warfare, and developing quantitative techniques in preparation for the coming digital age. MGB, in contrast, was pursuing the same applications and techniques it had developed during World War II. It was falling behind both in funding and in attracting bright employees.

During my year in Vicksburg, the Remote Area Conflict Section of the Defense Advanced Research Projects Agency (ARPA) funded the research at WES. During the same year, MGB acquired a new chief (whom I'll call George for now, and Nemesis later on), lost more funding, and underwent a major reduction in force.

I made a special trip to Washington to urge George to develop ties with ARPA, hoping to secure new research opportunities. George would have none of this. He wanted no involvement with ARPA. But his boss was enthused, and so the three of us went together to meet the director of Remote Area Conflict studies at the Pentagon. The meeting went well, and we picked up a small project for me to carry out after my assignment at WES: A feasibility study for an environmental research project on the salt deserts of Iran. Perhaps Iran was being recognized as a possible future site for a "war of national liberation." If this feasibility study succeeded, it was expected to lead into the larger study, making MGB once again relevant to the research goals of the modern world.

After I returned to Washington, completed the feasibility study, and submitted the manuscript to George, I saw something unusual for the Geological Survey: a manager making substantive changes to the researcher's findings. I read over these changes and accepted them. Too bad, for I completely missed the negative implications of one of his changes, to the effect that Iranian salt deserts are unique, and unlike any other deserts elsewhere in the world. That was true, of course, but I hadn't considered it particularly relevant to the issue at hand.

It was fully two years before that statement came back to haunt me. I was with a new employer and on assignment in the Middle East when I met one of the old-timers from ARPA. I asked whatever happened to the salt desert study. He said, "It's your fault. The ambassador killed the project because of what you said in your feasibility study. You and I both know those deserts are unique. That's why we needed the study so badly, because we've never fought in such places and we need to know a great deal about how their environment would affect military operations. But the ambassador doesn't think a research project is worthwhile unless it applies to the whole world."

Indeed, since then we have already found ourselves operating in those deserts, and we may not yet have seen the last of them.

In the short term, however, I stayed on with George for another 6 months, and then found employment in the fields I had been seeking – research on applications of geology in unconventional warfare. And, beyond anything I had ever wanted, the new job involved extensive field assignments in Vietnam and Iran.

NEMESIS

My new job was with a "think tank" named the Research Analysis Corporation, a private not-for-profit firm supported by contracts with the Department of Defense and other federal agencies. I joined the Unconventional Warfare Department, where they were finding many new applications of geology and terrain science in this type of warfare.

Every new job presents unanticipated problems, but I did enjoy being rid of George. But wait! I soon learned that George and I had changed jobs at the same time. He had moved into nothing less than the position of director of Remote Area Conflict studies at the Pentagon. He succeeded the very man he had been unwilling to talk with several months earlier! I never did figure out the personal politics of all this. Perhaps he foresaw his move to ARPA, and simply didn't want any connection with the Geological Survey in his new position. But it was clear – alas! – that he was now overseeing the contract of the department I worked in.

In me, he apparently saw possibilities for new kinds of projects, and he dealt directly with me while ignoring all the layers of bosses between us.

His first approach seemed innocuous, though unpleasant. He wanted me to evaluate a military environmental research project that had been underway for several years involving faculty and graduate students at a highly respected university. I found that its management had failed in a number of ways. The various parts of what should have been a unified approach had been studied separately, and by now were completely incompatible with each other. I explained my findings to the researchers and considered their points until we reached a conclusion that all of us considered fair.

Then I dutifully presented my report to George. He used it as a basis for discontinuing the project. I knew that was his intent all along, and that I was his chosen hatchet man. Such are the humilities we sometimes endure to make a living. By now I was well along in the transition from "George" to "Nemesis."

His next approach was a bit more troublesome. He discussed the problem of Viet Cong tunnels in Vietnam, and said that a research program was underway to help in detecting them. The project was now at the point where they needed to have a geologist – like me – look at the tunnels and observe their geologic settings. This could be useful in two ways: (1) predicting where tunneling might or might not be feasible; and (2) determining the types of soils, rocks, and moisture conditions that any detection apparatus would have to be designed for. George reminded me that our contract would soon be up for renewal, and said that I should keep this in mind if I had any problems with accepting the assignment.

I never refused a legitimate project assignment because of reasons like fearing or disliking it. I always pointed out, however, any concerns I had as to whether its goal could actually be achieved.

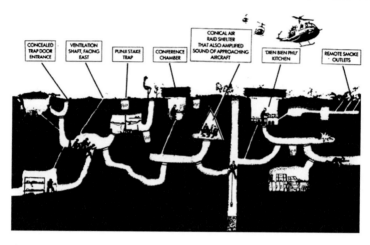

Representative layout for a tunnel complex, from U.S. Army training materials.

The problem I saw in this case was one of security. As soon as American forces secured an area and found tunnels, they searched the tunnels and then destroyed them completely. The best opportunities to examine tunnels in detail would be in areas currently being secured or not yet secured. I knew from previous experience that no responsible commander would allow a civilian employee to get on his bicycle and move alone into such places. Military escort would be required.

Which led to a further possibility: A military commander might say to me, "Look, I've got a war to fight here. We're busy, and we don't want to add to the risks we already have. Your little geologic field trips just aren't

important enough for us to fool with. Go back home."

I discussed this with George. He sent a cable to Saigon. They replied that I should proceed as planned. End of discussion. I went to Vietnam.

Only after arriving in Saigon, and getting to know the military folks there, did I learn that I had been a laughing stock even before arriving. George's cable had asked the question, "Can you guarantee the safety of this geologist?" In a war zone, yet!

II. The Main Event

GETTING STARTED

As soon as instructions from ARPA were received, RAC began preparations for the tunnel project. The project was too large and complex for one man to handle. Perry Narten, a geologist with whom I had collaborated on many previous projects, and a good friend as well, was assigned as my partner.

Perry and I arrived in Saigon on October 9, 1966.

Known today as Ho Chi Minh City, Saigon was at that time the capital of the Republic of Vietnam (South Vietnam). I understand that it had once been a beautiful city of about 50,000 people. Since then, it had undergone Japanese occupation, followed by twenty years of war involving French, American, and other allied forces opposing South Vietnamese insurgent groups and North Vietnamese troops. The city had endured war damage and the decay of buildings and infrastructure. With the addition of refugees, other displaced people, and soldiers, the population had swollen to about 2 million.

RAC maintained an apartment in a pleasant downtown neighborhood at 23 Gia Long. Perry and I joined the two occupants, Harry and Dorothy, for the length of our stay. The RAC field office, part of a larger compound of ARPA field offices, was a 15-minute walk from the apartment.

Saigon remained our base of operations, but through short trips we visited other places important to our mission, including Bien Hoa, Tay Ninh, and Cu Chi. We returned for a longer stay at Cu Chi, which became the primary focus of our field surveys. It was located about 20 miles northwest of Saigon.

Cu Chi was strategically significant because it controlled some of the principal land and water routes for infiltration of supplies from the Ho Chi Minh trail. Cu Chi and the Iron Triangle nearby were strongholds for the Viet Cong throughout the war. The accom-

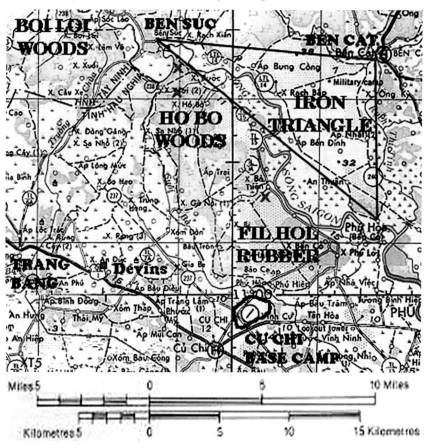

panying map shows these and other nearby areas, in which were found the greatest concentrations of tunnels in all of South Vietnam.

In January 1966, about one square mile of land was cleared for the construction of Camp Cu Chi, the headquarters of the U.S. 25th Infantry Division. Apparently it was not fully known at that time that the area was infested with Viet Cong tunnels. In ensuing months, surprise attacks occurred from inside the camp's perimeter. An eyewitness told me of seeing several VC suddenly appearing in the mess hall, firing machine guns. When Perry and I arrived at Cu Chi, this problem had finally been solved within the camp itself, but tunnels in the general area remained a hot issue. The ARPA officers urged us to concentrate on this area, and we did.

Camp Cu Chi, Headquarters of the 25th Infantry Division
Source: Danny Driscoll

LEARNING ABOUT TUNNELS

Following the events at Camp Cu Chi, American forces had accumulated a great deal of knowledge and experience with tunnels by late 1966. Under the standard one-year tour of duty in Vietnam, many soldiers who had experienced tunnel warfare were still in country.

The normal procedure, once a tunnel complex had been detected and pacified by a strong ground force, was to search it and then destroy it by shaped demolition charges. At first, regular infantry soldiers were assigned to the search. Many were killed during encounters with enemy soldiers and booby traps. The need for a Military Occupational Specialty (MOS) was soon recognized, and numerous training materials were produced. The trainees under this program, who I understood were all volunteers, have frequently been called "Tunnel Rats." My field notes suggest that "Tunnel Runners" was the more common term in use among the people I worked with. These runners were acknowledged as major American heroes of the war.

Backing up the above sources of information, extensive intelligence files on tunnels were built up in the 25th Division and in the headquarters of the Military Assistance Command, Vietnam (MACV).

Our ARPA project officer, naval Lieutenant Commander Richard M. Gowing, was quick and thorough in seeing that we made all the informational contacts needed for our project. Among the facts that we learned:

The greatest concentrations of tunnels were in the III Corps Tactical Zone, extending from the sea, through Saigon and Cu Chi, on to the Cambodian border, as depicted in the accompanying map. I saw the 1966 version of this map, which gave added in-

LOCATIONS OF MAJOR VC TUNNELS FOUND IN III CORPS TACTICAL ZONE UP TO JANUARY 1968 (Source: Confidential US Army map)

formation on the length of each tunnel or tunnel complex. Most of these were much less than one mile long; only a few exceptions approached or exceeded a length of one mile.

These lengths should be kept in mind in view of statements, partly true but misleading, that suggest the tunnels were much longer and were intended for long-distance travel. Examples of such information are: "they stretched from Saigon to the Cambodian border," "about 200 kilometers of tunnels were built," and "they were used to connect villages, districts, and provinces together so the fighters could move between areas undetected."

Estimating the numbers of tunnels runs into a problem of definition: They ranged in size from major headquarters facilities to "holes in the ground," and by this latter definition the number could approach 5,000. By more conventional definitions, such as squad-size tunnels and larger, the count was about 500 in late 1966, and rising each month.

In news accounts and training materials alike, chief emphasis has been placed on the larger complexes, which held such facilities as living areas, storage depots, ordnance factories, hospitals, headquarters, kitchens, and any other facility needed by an army. For these purposes, compartments were built to whatever dimensions the facility required. The largest of them required some form of lining and support.

Connecting tunnels, and those used for such purposes as scout observations, surprise sniper attacks, ambushes, and town control, did not require large dimensions. To ensure stability without lining or support, they normally ranged in width from 0.8 to 1.2 meters, and in height from 0.8 to 1.8 meters. The minimum roof thickness was 1.5 meters.

A diagram illustrating the typical layout of a major tunnel complex was presented in Part I. Another is presented here. Both are from U.S. Army training materials.

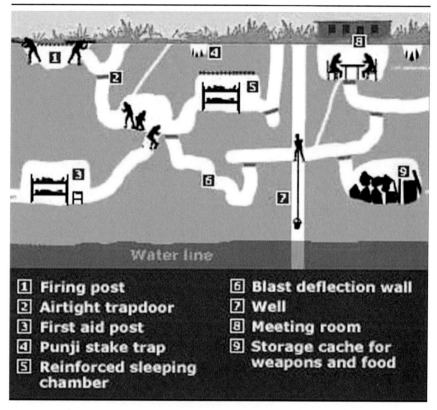

1. Firing post
2. Airtight trapdoor
3. First aid post
4. Punji stake trap
5. Reinforced sleeping chamber
6. Blast deflection wall
7. Well
8. Meeting room
9. Storage cache for weapons and food

No central entity designed the tunnels or oversaw their construction. They evolved in response to local needs and were constructed under the supervision of local Viet Cong leaders. Teams of local residents performed the labor of digging by hand. In many cases, each team worked only in a sector near its home village, and was unaware of extensions into neighboring sectors.

The early tunnels were dug as hiding places for the Viet Minh, a nationalist guerilla force that fought the Japanese during World War II and the French afterward until 1954. More tunnels were built later as pressure increased from American and South Vietnamese troops.

We learned various examples of digging rates, which varied according to the soil, the weather, and the health and skills of the labor force. Some of the rates cited were: one cubic meter per person per day; 50 meters of tunnel length per day for a team of 100 workers.

Fortitude and determination were needed not only in the construction of tunnels, but also in their use.

Soldiers had to maneuver through low, narrow passages interrupted by many twists, turns, and trap doors designed to minimize effects of underground blasts. Floors were frequently flooded during the wet season, and snakes and scorpions were also encountered. Trap door openings were tiny; some of those we observed measured as little as 12 by 18 inches.

Care was needed when moving around booby traps that had been placed to defend the tunnels. Among American soldiers, booby traps were responsible for 11% of the deaths and 17% of the woundings during the war. The traps ranged from simple punji stakes (sharpened bamboo, often smeared with excrement) and underfoot spike boards to various explosive devices.

Noteworthy among the explosive devices were Claymore Mines, a particularly deadly type of antipersonnel weapon. They consisted of round flat pans filled with plastic explosive, packed with nails or other small pieces of metal to serve as shrapnel. From a mine mounted in a forward-facing position, this shrapnel would shower a large area.

LEARNING ABOUT THE ENVIRONMENT

The goal of our project was to contribute to a multi-part study titled "A Systematic Approach to the Detection of VC Tunnels." Part I: Strategic and Tactical Factors was in preparation by Major H.W. Newbigin of the Australian Army, assisted by Lieutenant J.D. Harden of the U.S. Navy. We would prepare Part II: Environmental Factors. The two teams cooperated closely and exchanged information freely.

In Part II, our task was to match the information we had on tunnel locations with detailed descriptions of the environment, primarily geology, soils, and subsurface moisture and ground water conditions. We had two goals. One was to seek any association between tunnels and specific environmental settings, which might then guide search efforts. The other was to compile information on the properties of the natural materials and their changing moisture conditions, as an aid in the design of detection equipment.

Tunnels in the III Corps Tactical Zone were exclusively located in certain higher terrace levels of the geologic unit known as Old Alluvium. These were old floodplain deposits formed during previous higher stages of sea level. They were now elevated to several elevations up to about 70 feet above the current sea level.

They could readily be recognized by land use patterns on the uplands, consisting either of woodlands or of cultivated fields and hedgerows.

In soil science terminology, these materials were identified and mapped as grey podzolic soils and low-humic gley soils. Tunnels could be located freely anywhere in the first type, which lay at higher elevations. In the second type, at lower elevations, tunnels could be located only at selected sites on high ground. In lower areas, the ground water table was too shallow.

The soil materials were mostly clays with some silt and fine sand. They were "lateritic," meaning that iron content, leached from the upper layers, had accumulated in the lower layers as a cement. When thoroughly air-dried, those soils took on properties close to those of concrete, and were resistant to ever becoming soft and moist again. Finally, near the ground water table, still higher concentrations of iron produced layers of laterite pebbles and rocks, highly resistant to digging even by mechanized equipment. This set the depth limit for digging tunnels in the usual fashion, by hand. The limit typically varied between 10 and 20 meters.

The soils were highly stable without lining or support, depending, of course, on the size of the excavation. After drying out, they were known to withstand 40-pound cratering charges, hand grenades, and other explosives without collapsing. Their stability is evident in the following photos of a tunnel from which the roof had been removed.

Vietnam has a tropical monsoon climate. The south monsoon, May through September, features the single rainy season, with annual rainfall exceeding 1,000 mm almost everywhere. The north monsoon, October through April, brings dry and sunny weather to southern Vietnam, while rainfall is infrequent and light. In the Saigon area specifically, the rainy season tends to persist later, tapering off during the October-November period when we were there.

The rainy season was the best time for tunnel construction. During the dry season, the soils often became too dry and hard to be dug by hand. Along the interior tunnel surfaces, many areas of soil were so thoroughly air-dried that they were more or less permanently hardened and unlikely to regain moisture and softness. Trap doors in tunnels were normally built up of layers of wood and soil. Even though these were exposed to seasonal rains, soldiers sometimes mistook the soil for concrete.

As our study progressed, it became clear that tunnel locations in III Corps Tactical Zone were strictly confined to certain suitable soil and geologic situations as described above. Nevertheless, we were unable to meet our first goal. The suitable conditions were so widespread that they did not provide adequate guidance for organizing a search effort. We did succeed with our second goal, providing detailed data about ground conditions to assist in the design of sensing systems.

These widespread conditions were not only suitable for hand-dug tunnels; they were pre-eminently suitable in comparison with other situations around the world. This suggests that tunneling may have been an established tradition of Vietnamese culture through previous centuries. It would explain the speed and skill with which they employed it in times of occupation and war.

To support this speculation, it is worth noting that China once had such a tradition, taking advantage of widespread deposits of loess (windblown silt and clay). Loess was well suited for digging artificial caves, though it lacked the cements that gave the Vietnamese soils added stability. The Shaanxi earthquake of 1556 was the deadliest earthquake in history, owing to the fact that millions of people were living in caves dug in the loess. Many of the dwellings collapsed, and the toll was estimated at 830,000 deaths.

FINDING A TUNNEL

Note: An account of this event, in a letter dated November 3. 1966, is presented in Part III: Letters from the Front. The purpose here is to summarize that account and to fill in some of the gaps.

Camp Cu Chi, headquarters of the 25th Infantry Division, was approximately one square mile in area. It was largely surrounded by hostile territory and was aptly termed a front-line camp. Its perimeter was lined by barbed wire, machine gun bunkers, and artillery

emplacements. Every night the guns were fired repeatedly, flares were dropped, and in general sleep was frequently interrupted.

My longest visit to the camp began on October 31, when the 25th Division had scheduled an operation to check out the report by a VC prisoner about a tunnel located near Ap Cho, about 3 miles southeast of the camp. The operation would be carried out by Charlie Company, 1st Battalion, 5th Infantry Regiment (Mechanized), under the command of Captain Blair. When I arrived, six armored personnel carriers (APCs) were lined up ready to make the trip. A helicopter waited nearby for Captain Blair, who would lead the operation from the air.

Soon the VC prisoner was brought forward. He was a young

man, neat and clean. He wore the black pajama uniform that I had heard of but had never seen. His hands were tied behind his back, and while in Camp Cu Chi he was blindfolded. He was docile. His face never showed any emotion.

The prisoner was interviewed through an interpreter. At the site we would visit, he had been foreman over a work force of 100 diggers using picks and shovels. A North Vietnamese army officer had given him plans for his sector of the tunnel complex. From 1961, some digging was done each wet season, normally at a rate of 50 meters per day. The ground was too hard for digging in the dry season. The entire complex was unlined, except for the room just inside the main entry, where the roof was only about 1 foot thick. He claimed that the entire length of the tunnel complex was about 1 kilometer, which would be one of the longest on record.

Proceeding from the camp, our column crossed paddy fields (flooded fields where rice is grown). Here we avoided the small roads on the dikes because they might be mined. Instead, we plowed through the rice in a scene very similar to that shown below, which came from a picture post card. The soldiers mostly rode on the top decks of the APCs, while I chose a bench seat in the interior.

On the roads, a sizable group of Vietnamese civilians moved along with us, frequently cheering and waving. Soon a brisk trade

was set up in refreshments for the troops, mostly soft drinks and bananas. I wasn't sure where these people came from; a large area here had been cleared of all inhabitants the previous February.

The most comical scene occurred when we had left the crowds and moved into a deserted area. Along came a boy riding a bicycle on the cart track. He and the soldiers struck up a conversation, and it soon developed that he had a bunch of bananas hidden in his basket. So the bargaining started. For a can of C rations and 20 piasters (17 cents) he waded over and gave us the bananas. We all enjoyed them because we were parched.

Presently, I heard the sound of gunfire. As I quickly learned, we had encountered two VC in a sampan in a canal. One was killed, the other captured. The captured one was tied up and dumped unceremoniously into the APC, where he sat staring at me from about three feet away. He wore no uniform. I asked one of the officers how they knew he was a VC. "Because he tried to get away when he saw us coming."

Meanwhile, the prisoner leading us to the tunnel was lost for a long time and we went in circles. I was beginning to wonder whether they might punish him for leading us on a wild goose chase. But finally he recognized a familiar tree and led us right to the tunnel opening.

The trap door at the entry was wide open, as were two others inside the tunnel. This indicated that we had probably surprised someone inside. The entry door closely resembled the one in the picture.

When I approached it and noted the size of the opening, about 12 by 18 inches, I declared, "I'm not going in. This tunnel isn't built for a man of my caliber." Of course, I already knew that Capt. Blair wouldn't allow me to go in.

Those who went in were a couple of young soldiers, trained as tunnel runners, who seemed absolutely fearless. They went far into the tunnel, digging their way through a collapsed area. Movements by an APC caused a repeat of the collapse, which they protested, using their only contact with the surface – a phone on a long line. They found important items in the tunnel. At one collapsed place they found large amounts of ammunition, Claymore mines (round pan-shaped objects in the photo), and many maps and documents, which included names of VC living in a nearby village. Chances are that those people were forewarned. Little boys kept hanging around

the tunnel site. When soldiers chased them, they climbed a tree to watch. The accompanying photos show the soldiers displaying their "loot."

There was an abandoned well nearby with fresh footprints on the clay walls, about 20 feet of murky water in it. The brave tunnel runners went all the way to the bottom, seeking additional tunnel

entrances. No diving apparatus – fully clothed, they just took a deep breath and jumped in, head first. They tied telephone wire around their waists so that we could pull them back up if necessary. Only one went in at a time, since the well was only about 2½ feet in diameter. Like many wells, this one was connected with chambers of the tunnel. Sometimes this presented the hazard of enemy troops in hiding, but not this time.

A couple of days after this operation, Captain Blair invited Perry and me to go out with his company on another operation, into the Iron Triangle. The area was of great interest, but we declined because (1) the operation would last 3 to 5 days. (2) the area was so infested with VC that the operation was preceded by heavy B-52 bombardment, very likely having destroyed tunnels and near-surface soils. And (3) the danger was still so great that they wanted us to work separately so that we couldn't both get hit at the same time.

That did it! We said thanks but no thanks.

RESULTS OF OUR STUDY

As previously mentioned, Perry and I were unable to meet the first goal of our study. The soil and geologic conditions most favorable for tunnel construction were so widespread that they offered little useful guidance for planning search efforts.

We did accomplish our second goal, to describe the properties of earth materials that would be useful in the design of detection systems. We had in mind various techniques of exploration geophysics, including seismic methods, ground-penetration radar, remote sensing, and several others.

This goal was a limited one, however, because two men without laboratory support can do only so much in two months. We had done the basic work, but we realized that more detailed follow-on surveys would be needed before final designs could be made.

On October 26, I was pleased to learn that the follow-on surveys were in the works. A team would visit the ARPA field office in

December to arrange for the next phase, beginning in January 1967. The Air Force would make flights to test remote sensing techniques. A ground team from the Waterways Experiment Station (WES) of the Corps of Engineers would conduct field surveys for three months, traveling widely throughout the study area, the III Corps Tactical Zone.

I knew these people from WES. I had recently completed a year working with them in Vicksburg on a joint research program. I knew that they had the backup of a state-of-the-art soils analysis laboratory, and that they had developed brilliant techniques for mapping soils, portraying a variety of their quantitative properties. They were well qualified.

The ARPA project officer and I were much concerned about one problem, though: Traveling in the back country. Perhaps they didn't know what they were getting into. One didn't wander around the countryside here as they had done in Thailand. And in the hottest part of the year yet, poor fellows.

There was no further news of the project until several months later. In January, I learned that the Air Force mission was "curtailed," and the ground mission was delayed. Sometime later, I learned that the field team had arrived, had traveled to Camp Cu Chi, and then never managed to get outside the camp's perimeter. With the failure of this work, it was clear that any design of detection systems would not move ahead. I was distressed to hear that we were moving into a new phase, which I called The Final Solution.

THE FINAL SOLUTION

By 1969, the tunnels had made significant contributions to the communist cause. In that year, they were finally destroyed for all time by B-52 carpet bombing raids. The first photo below shows a B-52-D dropping a string of 750-pound bombs. The second view, unfortunately of poor quality, shows the crater left by the detonation of just one bomb. From these photos, one can judge the extent

of environmental destruction. Carpet bombing was used in every area where there was any suspicion of tunnels.

As presented by Ramon W. Almodovar and J. David Rogers in their training materials on The Tunnels of Cu Chi, General William Westmoreland was quoted as saying "No one has ever demonstrated more ability to hide his installations than the Viet Cong; they were human moles." And the authors concluded:

The VC demonstrated resolve by outlasting the Americans. Although no American unit of even squad size or greater ever surrendered to the Viet Cong or North Vietnamese during the entire Vietnam War, they still managed to prevail."

The training materials have been of great value in the preparation of this book.

III. *Letters from the Front*

The letters were addressed to family members including my wife, Jaquelin; my sons Jasper (then age 14), David (12), and Philip (9); and my mother, Edith.

FIRST...

SOME
OF THE
HIGHLIGHTS

October 10, 1966

Dear Jackie, Jasper, David, Philip, & Mom,

In Saigon the first thing noticed is the heat and humidity. Despite it all, the Vietnamese women dress gracefully and always look clean and fresh; I can't quite say the same for the men.

The next impression is that of all the military activity. Jeeps with machine guns sat on the runway as we deplaned. Soldiers all over, and the way they are packed in both living and working quarters is incredible. Last evening the sky was full of flares and helicopters, occasional jets. This morning it was artillery rather than the alarm that woke me up just before dawn. I rarely photograph military subjects; it could cause trouble.

The streets of Saigon are humming with traffic and pedestrians. Americans walk freely at all times except after the 11 pm curfew. The sights are like pictures out of a geography book – the people wear "coolie" hats, operate chicken barbecues in the middle of the sidewalk, etc. It has rained 3 or 4 times since I got here, but no problem – everyone just gets wet and then dries out as much as the humidity will allow.

October 20, 1966

Dear David,

This town is full of soldiers — not only traveling around, but on almost every block there is one sitting behind sandbags with a rifle or machine gun ready. Lots of barbed wire barricades on the sidewalk, so we have to walk in the street around them. Last night must have been a bad one outside of town. Around ten o'clock the guns started booming, the pom-poms were chattering, helicopters were buzzing around and dropping flares, and once in while it sounded like VC mortar shells in the distance. Yet everything looks innocent and peaceful by day.

October 21, 1966

Dear Mom,

This city is large in crowds (about 2,000,000), small in conveniences, dirty, and has very much the appearance of war. Sandbags, barbed wire, and armed guards all over the place. Apparently it was a beautiful place once when it held only about 50,000 people. But now it is jammed with refugees, not to mention troops, and little shacks have gone up all over and the original nice big buildings seem to be decaying rapidly.

There are some deterrents to roving the town and sightseeing, imposed by (1) Poor sanitation and the considerable danger of polluted food and water, except in a few trusted restaurants. (2) The general problem of not knowing a single word of the language. (3) The apparent lack of genteel entertainment places. (Movies seem to be shown in real fleabags, and are in French and Chinese only; the bars and nightclubs seem to be largely cutthroat joints), and (4) lack of security in outlying areas.

October 23, 1966

Dearest Jackie, Jasper, David and Philip:

While I'm still adapting to the climate, I find it weakening. I'm worn out every night by about 9 or 10. Tonight I could hardly stay awake at the restaurant, and it is not yet 9 and I think I'll start for bed when I finish this letter. The heat itself hasn't been too bad the last few days (upper 80's) but the humidity is unbelievable. The housekeeper washed my fatigue trousers 2 days ago and they're still on the line (under porch roof), soaking wet. Also all our bath towels are wet, so tonight we have them spread out under a ceiling fan trying to dry them.

Saigon has a new waterworks which promises, according to the paper, "disease-free water in six months", but meanwhile I drink wine, coke, or beer. At the apartment, the housekeeper boils water, then strains it through cotton for drinking, cooking, tooth brushing, etc.

October 24, 1966

Dear Jasper,

I'm taking pictures whenever there's an opportunity, but there haven't been too many. Two problems: The city is so much like a military camp I'm afraid of photographing something I shouldn't, and either getting shot at or getting arrested. Also, there are so many sights of poor people on the streets. I'm afraid they may be offended.

On the first point, to show you how nervous sentries are around here, two Vietnamese were riding a motor scooter a couple of blocks from here the other day when it stalled right in front of an American BOQ (Bachelor Officers' Quarters). The MPs (military police) yelled to move on, and when they didn't move for a few seconds, the MPs started shooting at them. Fortunately they missed, then they found out the riders were two South Vietnamese Army lieutenants in civilian clothes. After that the MPs were so upset that they barricaded the street for the rest of the day.

October 27, 1966

Dear Jackie,

Saigon is beginning to look festive in anticipation of the national day, November 1. Banners all over, military bands practicing. This evening I walked to the PX and almost dropped my teeth to find myself engulfed by hundreds of young men and women, late teens and early 20's I guess, pouring out of several big open trucks. They all were wearing black pajamas—the customary VC uniform—and to top it off they all were waving red flags. I thought the moment of VC victory had come. Later they paraded down the street. Haven't figured them out yet, but it was all very peaceful and within 200 feet of the heavily guarded U.S. Bachelor Officers' Quarters (BOQ).

I'm polishing some of the rust off my French. The Vietnamese are all (as far as I've met them) pretty poor in English, but many are fluent in French. So French has gotten me over a few crucial communication problems. There is still a small colony of French business people living here, but I understand the Vietnam government is giving them the boot as fast as it can. They recently revoked licenses of French doctors, even though doctors are badly needed here.

October 28, 1966

Dearest Jackie:

I get an inkling that things are not so good here in the Vietnamese government. No details, except that a bunch of ministers tried to resign just before the Manila meeting. Seems to be trouble between native South Vietnamese and the large number of North Vietnamese (by origin, not politically) that have important posts here, including Prime Minister Ky himself.

Of course all the news here is heavily censored—lots of blank columns in the newspaper, and once in a while American magazines like Time fail to get through, even to the PX. So let me know if you've heard more about this than I have.

October 30, 1966

Dearest Jackie, Jasper, David, Philip, and Mom:

It was three weeks ago today when I arrived in Saigon. We have worked every day since then, including Saturdays and Sundays. Today, though, we gave up about 2:00 PM, ate, and took the rest of the day off. This consisted of wandering around town, getting film at the PX; and then I heard a band playing and went to find a US Marine Band concert in progress, apparently dedicating a new statue in front of the National Assembly building—a statue honoring the South Vietnamese soldiers.

Tomorrow morning we are driving to Cu Chi again –about 25 mi. NW of Saigon, where we will stay at an Army Camp, 25th Division Headquarters, for 3 to 5 days. That is an area of numerous tunnels and from there they will take us out to do the fieldwork. They are the people who are so experienced with tunnels, the people we met before who had crawled through many of them.

This trip will put us out of Saigon during the national holiday, probably just as well. They have built big grandstands where the dignitaries, Vietnamese and American, will view the parade. We ask ourselves half-jokingly how many mines are planted under those grandstands. It may turn out not to be a joke.

Had a scare a couple of nights ago. The VC were attacking a U.S. ammunition dump and apparently the third mortar shell hit home. There was an ungodly explosion. It was 9 PM and Perry and

National Assembly building

I were walking down the street near here. I could have sworn it was a block or two away. As it turns out, the dump was 11 miles outside of Saigon, at Bien Hoa. Broke windows even in the city.

Please keep your mind at peace about us over here. Even though you may hear of violent incidents, they are probably less frequent here than auto accidents in Washington. And people react to the incidents in about the same way, no more, no less, as Washingtonians react to auto accidents. We are taking every precaution.

November 2, 1966

Dearest Jackie:

This is being written from Camp Cu Chi. We left Saigon 9 am Monday the 31st, arrived here about 11 am. We learned that a VC prisoner had told of a tunnel near here, so we joined with a company that went out Monday afternoon to find it. Did so and returned there yesterday to spend the day.

Today we spent our time within the camp. It had been infested with tunnels before it was occupied, so we went around sampling soils and spent a good bit of time at a well they are digging here.

November 3, 1966

Dearest Jackie:

Camp Cu Chi is the headquarters of the 25th Infantry Division, probably some 10,000 men more or less. The camp is spread out over perhaps a square mile. It is pretty well surrounded by hostile territory, and is aptly termed a front-line camp. It is surrounded by barbed wire, machine gun bunkers, and artillery emplacements.

There were no incidents within the camp while I was there, but every night the guns banged away, flares were dropped, and in general sleep was frequently interrupted. We picked a good time to be there, for as I mentioned I was glad to be out of Saigon on Tuesday, their national holiday. We feared the VC might try something, and they did. In addition to numerous grenades in the city, there were two bombardments by recoilless rifles (something like bazookas or small rockets) that were aimed at the parade area.

Several holes were put in the roof of the Grall hospital across the street from our apartment, and one went through the wall of the building next door, breaking glass in the far end of our building and putting lots of shrapnel holes in cars parked out front, including the one we rent. Our address is 23 Gia Long, and some of the press dispatches made specific mention of it.

Harry and Dorothy were walking to the parade, about 100 yards down the street, when the shells hit and they are still pretty scared. It seems Perry and I were much safer on the front lines. Harry and

Dorothy have been here a long time, so you can see from their excitement over this that it's most unusual—probably represents a VC maximum effort for the occasion of the holiday.

When we got to Cu Chi, the 25th Division was planning an operation that afternoon to check out the report of a VC prisoner on a tunnel located about 3 or 4 miles southeast of the camp. The main body of troops, about a company, went by armored personnel carriers (APCs, something like tanks) while a few flew helicopter support. We were in one of the APCs. The only enemy encountered were two VC in a sampan (boat) who tried to get away when they saw us; one was killed, the other captured. The captured one wore no uniform; I asked one of the officers how they knew the man was a VC. "Because he tried to get away when he saw us coming."

During parts of the trip, both he and the other VC prisoner, the one who was leading us to the tunnel, were riding with us in the APC and rubbing elbows with us. Completely pacified & docile—but hands tied anyway. Our prisoner guide was lost for a long time and we went in circles. I was beginning to fear they might punish him for leading us on a wild goose chase through paddy fields, hedgerows, brush. But finally he recognized a familiar tree and led us right to the tunnel opening. Door was wide open, as were several trap doors inside. Pits nearby with sharpened bamboo stakes in them. The significance of the open doors was that we had probably just surprised someone inside.

Perry and I did not go into the tunnel. This was done by a couple of young soldiers called tunnel rats or tunnel runners who seemed absolutely fearless. There was an abandoned well nearby with fresh footprints on the clay walls, about 20 feet of murky water in it. So our brave tunnel runners went under the water seeking additional tunnel entrances. No diving apparatus—fully clothed, they just took a deep breath and jumped in. Tied telephone wire around their waists so that we could pull them back up if necessary. Only one went in at a time, since the well was only about 2½ feet in diameter. They placed some people out on ambush around the tunnel for the night, and then returned to their forward encampment, while we lucky ones took helicopter back to Camp Cu Chi for the night.

The author, about to fly back to Camp Cu Chi for the night.
He is the passenger, not the pilot.

Returned next morning, spent rest of day sampling soils and finding new tunnel entrances. Where the vehicles went over a tunnel they collapsed it. Unfortunately this happened while the tunnel runners were in there, but they dug out successfully. At one collapsed place they found large amounts of ammunition, "Claymore" mines, and many maps and documents, including names of VC in the nearby village. Their goose is cooked. Chances are, though, that they were forewarned, because neighborhood kids kept hanging around—when soldiers chased them they climbed a tree to watch.

The area was once heavily settled but is now like a no man's land – no idea where these kids came from. One of the funniest episodes: We were plowing through flooded paddy land, avoiding the small cart tracks on the dikes because these might be mined, and seemingly miles from nowhere, when along comes a boy on a bicycle on the cart track! He and the soldiers strike up a conversation, and it soon develops that he has a bunch of bananas hidden in his basket. So the bargaining starts. For a can of C rations and 20 piasters (17 cents) he waded over to us and gave us the bananas, which we all enjoyed because we were parched. Talk about the Good Humor man at the front lines!

Yesterday we sampled soils around Camp Cu Chi, while the troops we had been with finished exploring the tunnel. Today we were invited to go out with them on another operation. The area was of great interest, but we chickened out because (1) the operation would last 3 to 5 days. (2) The area was so VC–infested that the operation was preceded by heavy B-52 bombardment, which we saw from the camp early this morning, and (3) the danger was still great enough that they wanted us to work separately so we couldn't both get hit at once.

That did it! We said thanks but no thanks.

November 6, 1966

Dearest Jackie,

You remember we were invited to go along on a second operation out of Cu Chi with the same people we accompanied Monday and Tuesday. I understand they are having a rough time on that operation—one armored personnel carrier blown up the first day. Tay Ninh, the place we visited Thursday, had a big attack Friday morning.

This war is terribly deceiving because one moment all seems peaceful, the next all hell breaks loose.

...AND NOW,

THE REST
OF THE
LETTERS

FIRST IMPRESSIONS

October 9, 1966

Dearest Jackie:

It is 6:30 Sunday morning here in Hong Kong, and I figure it is 5:30 Saturday afternoon for you. The sky is just beginning to turn pink in the east. I try to picture what you are doing, and can imagine you are putting away some shopping bags while Jimmy is reading, David working in the basement, and Philip outside riding his bike!

October 11, 1966

Dearest Jackie, Jasper, David, and Philip,

Went out to one of the offices near Tan Son Nhut airfield — that's the main Saigon airfield, where I arrived — to see some American military intelligence people.

Their office is a building about the size of our local firehouse, but over 500 people work in it. An old warehouse; no windows, but a few window air conditioners have been stuck through the wall. They make it just bearable inside, but the air is still warm and humid enough that the cold blast from the units makes a fog like your breath in cold weather.

When I left the office, I asked the Vietnamese driver to take me by the main terminal building at Tan Son Nhut airfield, so that I could see whether our footlockers had arrived.

The office and the terminal building weren't far apart. They were in view of each other. But the main runway stood between them. Going around the runway would add a couple of miles to our trip, and the driver would have none of that. He drove up to the runway at a point where an American soldier was on guard, manning a machine gun. With gestures, the soldier made it clear that we were not to cross the runway.

Well, the driver waited and waited until the soldier was distracted, and then he gunned the auto for all it was worth. We practically flew across to the terminal. The whole way, I wondered what a machine gun bullet in the back would feel like. But I guess my American presence made the guard think twice before shooting.

There are little lizards (geckoes?) here that would remind you of the "chameleons" (anolis) in Mississippi, only grayer. They live in the house with us. Some on the ceilings, one behind the bathroom mirror, etc. Each one seems to have his permanent territory and nobody bothers them because all they do is eat insects — a good thing!

On the street corner beneath our veranda are a couple of sidewalk stalls where they sell food — there are always 20 to 50 people gathered about, standing or sitting on the sidewalk, eating. We call it the local Howard Johnson's. Big fight there this evening between

two women. They never came to blows but the shrieks could be heard all through our apartment. A couple of wagons sell food and it is cooked right there on little buckets of charcoal. Across the street from "Howard Johnson's" is the Grall Hospital.

It seems wherever there's a muddy pond — something you wouldn't put your toe in — there are several little boys swimming, diving, and splashing. They must have antibodies for everything. But they do seem to be learning to boil their drinking water. I often see men pulling water carts, and occasionally at Howard Johnson's they seem to be boiling it and selling it to people who come with thermos jugs.

October 13, 1966

Dearest Jackie,

I believe yesterday was our hottest day so far — 95 degrees F. And, as you'll recall from Vicksburg, that can be fierce when the humidity is high. It cools very little at night, and as a result the air conditioner sort of lost the battle last night. Rain showers this afternoon helped a good bit.

Ai Lin and her children

Our housekeeper, Ai Lin, had a fall a couple of weeks ago in the market — slipped on a banana or something. Has been feeling poorly since. Worked as usual yesterday but got in a bit late this morning. She sent two of her daughters to get breakfast, but she was on the job when we came home for lunch.

Dorothy Clark talked privately with her a while and came out with the news that she'd had a miscarriage at 3 months — presumably last night! She asked Dorothy to get her some champagne to make her feel better. She has to pay $15.00 for it on the black market, but we can get it for about $1.00. The average Vietnamese income is about $200.00 per year. Here are pictures of Ai Lin and two of her charming children.

EXPLORING

October 14, 1966

Dearest Jackie,

Tomorrow morning we are driving out to Bien Hoa — I guess 15 miles or so from Saigon — to a military field headquarters to see about likelihood of fieldwork. It's a busy 4-lane highway from here to there, but I believe we'll have armed guards for the trip anyway. Several others, including 3 officers, will accompany us.

October 16, 1966

Dear Philip,

I took a long trip today to visit an Army camp (Cu Chi) up near the front lines. We drove through many little villages that were interesting. At some of their houses the whole yard was a pond where they grew rice, kept ducks, fished, and swam.

At the Army camp they had some big guns that kept firing every few minutes at something about 5 miles away. Every time they fired the ceiling and the lights shook and rattled. I talked to many soldiers who'd had bad times with the Viet Cong. Some of them had gone into tunnels to catch enemy soldiers. The VC are small men and I understood that I was too big to go in. I am glad of that because they said there were snakes and lots of ants and scorpions in them.

Some of the tunnels were inside the Army camp, and until they found them, enemy soldiers used to sneak right into the middle of the camp. It is a nasty war here and our men are very brave. They  do many things, like crawling in tunnels, that many South Vietnamese soldiers are unwilling to do.

We came to a place where a bridge had been blown up several nights before, and there was a great big traffic jam to get over a pontoon bridge they had built. The new bridge was being guarded by two tanks.

October 16, 1966

Dear Jackie,

The account of my trip in Philip's letter may cause you some concern, but I really feel we were in safe hands. The road was crawling with U.S. soldiers the whole way, and the camp was a large Division Headquarters, not a little outpost. They have a "demonstration" tunnel up there — one that is captured and safe and is used for training new soldiers. We'll probably go up to have a look at it when (and if) our field equipment comes, but this body size restriction is real and I fully expect to work only on the surface. The Vietnamese are tiny people and only the smaller U.S. soldiers — volunteers — go into the tunnels.

FROM DAY TO DAY

October 19, 1966

Dear Jackie:

We are making progress thanks to the help and information we've been getting in Saigon. I don't think we'll come up with any startling conclusions because the problem is a very difficult one. These tunnels can be built in too many different kinds of places. And with the dense vegetation, the problem of the soldiers is that they are practically standing on the things before they realize it — and then all sorts of nasty things happen to them.

October 20, 1966

Dear David

Mama asked about evening entertainment here, so you can tell her about this. One night recently I went to a cocktail party, which I told about. All the other nights go like this:

There are four of us in the apartment. We get home about 5:45

PM. We sit and read for about an hour until supper is served. Then we sit down again for the rest of the evening and either read, write letters, or stare into space. Hardly anyone ever says anything the whole time. Once in a while when I get bored and want to make a really gay night of it, I sit alone out on the veranda and look down at the people on the street. Then somewhere between 9:30 and 10:30 I decide it's time to stop all this dissipating so I take a shower and go to bed.

The sound of "fireworks" then lulls me to sleep. Don't you envy me? All the movies here are either in Chinese or French. Frankly, I don't want to go into a theater. I think they're good places to pick up lice, bedbugs, thieves, and everything else. One of these evenings I may try a real night on the town, provided I have enough safe company, but somehow I don't think I'm missing much.

October 21, 1966

Dearest Jackie,

The last time I checked at the airport about the footlockers, I learned something about "personal space" differences between Vietnamese and Americans. When I got in line, there were about 100 people ahead of me. Gradually I worked forward, and just as I got to the head of the line, the man had to leave his post briefly. I leaned forward, resting my elbow and forearm on the counter.

When the man returned, I opened my mouth to say something, but heard only a squeaky little voice that seemed to come from my chest. I looked down, and there was a tiny Vietnamese woman who had broken in ahead of me by moving into the crook of my elbow! So I waited for my turn, and learned once again that the lockers had not arrived.

October 24, 1966

Dear David:

In answer to your questions on Vietnam:

Things are still pretty messy in Vietnam, but you'd never guess it to look at the people on the streets of Saigon. They have had this kind of war for 20 years now, and they have just learned to live as normally as possible despite it.

I have not ridden in a rickshaw. They are called pedicabs here, and all are driven by a man riding behind on what resembles the back half of a bicycle. (Some are motorized, as in this picture.) For this reason, the passenger sits out in front, and with the heavy traffic and crazy driving here, I'm scared to get in one. The regular rickshaw, which is pulled by a man on foot, is not seen here but I did see a lot of them in Hong Kong.

The lizards have not shown any dewlap (the neck swelling that we've seen on anolis "chameleons"), but they sometimes do make sort of a chirping sound—"chin-chuck", and that's their name. I just checked one on the bathroom ceiling, and he's grayish brown. Sometimes they turn to a light gray. They are just about the size of the green anolis and about the same shape.

The war sounds at night are not very scary because they sound far away, like distant thunder. They never seem to miss a night, but some nights are worse than others, and the windows rattle. We can hear one bang when a cannon goes off, then another bang when the shell hits.

October 24, 1966

Dear Philip:

You asked how we fitted into that building with 500 people. The answer is: Very tightly. It was a 1-story warehouse but they put in an extra floor, so now there are many places where tall men can't even stand up straight in it.

Children start to school here at the age of 5. They seem to have great big classrooms. We were walking on the street yesterday and had to wait while several classes walked past us in column. Each teacher must have had about 75 children. They are dressed just like kids at home, and they act just like them too.

You would really fit right in place on your bicycle here. The streets are full of thousands of people on bikes. Most of them are too poor to have a car. A good many have motorbikes (Hondas) and motor scooters. They are "oil-burners" and the streets are always full of heavy smoke.

November 5, 1966

Dear Mom:

We aren't allowed by the U.S. authorities to have any U.S. money except pennies. Had to turn it all in at the airport on arrival, in exchange for military currency, which is used in all U.S. establishments here and can be converted into Vietnamese money (piasters) as well. The military currency is all paper in denominations from 5 cents up—so the wallet gets awfully fat.

The apartment has a bathroom, kitchen with refrigerator & range, 2 bedrooms, living room and dining room. On 4th floor (actually, the fifth; by French custom, the ground floor isn't counted).

The address is 23 GIA LONG.

The bombing you heard about, 11 miles from Saigon, was the explosion of an ammunition dump at Bien Hoa. It wasn't bombed from the air — apparently either was hit by mortar fire or somebody carried in a package of explosives. I was walking on the street at the time and could have sworn it was only a block or two away. I was told that the door of our office flew open. I went over the site Thursday by helicopter and took a picture of a tremendous crater, 30 ft deep and over 150 ft wide.

The enclosed picture isn't a very good one, but I guess the best that can be expected. Dorothy Clark is the one on the left, and I suppose you recognize Perry on the right. Taken today at lunchtime.

November 7, 1966

Dearest Jackie,

The Navy Lieutenant Commander who is our project officer here has sort of a miserable routine. He eats breakfast and lunch at officer's mess, which is nothing but an overcrowded snack bar. Then

when he gets home in evening — his room on sixth floor walk-up —
he takes a can of something to eat alone in his room because he's too
tired to go back down again. He's in for a full year of that; has been
here since early June.

SIGNS OF WAR

November 9, 1966

Dearest Jackie,

Apparently the fighting that started near Tay Ninh the day after
we were there has resumed again. It went on about 3 days, then the
tide turned and the VC ran away. Now it seems the Americans have
caught up with them 17 miles from town and are giving them a bad
time.

*Vicinity of Tay Ninh. In the background, Ba Den (Black Virgin)
Mountain. At the time, Americans held its peak and lower slopes.
Communist forces held the middle slopes.*

One bright side—the VC seem to be defecting at about a rate of
500 a week. And those who are captured don't seem fanatic like the
Japanese of World War II. Once captured, the VC give in and some-

times even seem helpful afterward. Gives one the feeling that the situation could be brought under control if we could only stop the endless in-pouring of men and supplies from North Vietnam, much of it through the back country of Laos and Cambodia. By the way, I saw a bit of Cambodia in the distance as we flew over Tay Ninh.

November 10, 1966

Dear Jackie,

There is a big fuss in Saigon because the government is clamping down on the black market. Sidewalks on the main drags are cluttered with little stands selling all sorts of PX-type stuff stolen from the ships. They've been given 10 days or so to close up. The poor peddlers say they're in heavy debt for the merchandise and they need two months to sell it; they say they had no idea it was illegal, and I can believe them. The big shots who stole the stuff and sold it to them, of course, aren't touched. I suspect some of the big shots are French. There are still a number of Frenchmen around here—they mix with Americans like oil and water, and the Vietnamese are plenty anxious to get rid of them. A decree just came out closing some public schools that are still operated by the French.

November 11, 1966

Dearest Jackie,

The writing is still proceeding but it is painfully slow because we have so many bits of data—well logs & like—to check, compare, and correlate before making a statement. One other thing is worrying me a bit. I'm afraid some of the writing is going to have to be heavily edited and maybe even partly rewritten, and

I may have to do it. I'll have to feel my way slowly on this one. This stage of the work is certainly trying my patience. It's something I never had to do on my other field assignments — where I pushed through the fieldwork but didn't worry about a report until I got home.

MORE IMPRESSIONS

November 14, 1966

Dearest Jackie:

Only one new impression of the place recently—the boys will get a kick out of it: Right in the heart of town, by the waterfront, there is a traffic circle with a beautiful big pond full of fish and tropical water plants. There are always people fishing there (tiny black goldfish!) and a dozen kids or so splashing around the way they do in front of the Union Station. Well, usually at least one or two of the kids is completely bare—about the ages of Philip & David. I've taken a picture or two of the pool, but I haven't had the nerve to aim at the nudies what with all the people around as in a public park.

The black market people got the delay they asked for. They have two months to sell out. Also, the day after the government announced closing the French schools, they took it all back. Crazy doings. Now Prime Minister Ky is blasting corruption in the Port Authority. Chances are he'll shoot some corrupt official to set an example.

November 17, 1966

Dear Philip:

The area around here is one of the world's big rubber producers. There are immense plantations of rubber trees. They cut big gashes in the bark of the tree and collect the milky-looking sap that runs out. When that is heated over a fire it turns into latex, which is the main ingredient that the different kinds of rubber are made from.

November 22, 1966

Dear Mom,

The people here seem to be happy with very little. The lame (very few of these in evidence), the wounded, and those who are caught in the battlefields are the ones I feel most sorry for. But the general picture is one of "life as normal", with Americans seeming to take the war much more seriously than the Vietnamese. I suspect that most of the Vietnamese would just like to be left alone.

A most interesting friend of Harry & Dorothy stopped by apartment this evening. Dick Fisher, former Army engineer, retired Brigadier General. Now is assistant to the president of Air America, a private airline that does contract work for the U.S. military, and I think also the CIA.

He goes all over Southeast Asia building airfields. Told about one place where they built an airfield in 8 days under constant fire from VC. They had to get people in by helicopter, dropping almost straight down but with zigzags. Fifty-six of the labor force were killed and more then a hundred wounded.

He told of one airfield where they had to use the only local labor, the women of the VC, to tamp the runway with sections of logs. Had to pay the VC chief a "tribute" for this service, also a tax or toll on each vehicle that brought in heavy equipment by road. The VC knew the airfield would be used against them, but they wanted the money. Another place where he ran into graft: A Vietnamese province chief wanted about ten times what the land for the airfield was worth, so they didn't build there.

HOMEWARD BOUND

November 24, 1966

Dearest Jackie,

This morning about 11:30 we finished the report. The secretary still has the better part of a day's job typing the last few pages, inserting references & figure numbers etc. but at least it was in good enough shape that we gave a carbon of it to the ARPA project officer to read over. He came back late this afternoon to say he thought it was a fine report. So there's a small something to be thankful for today.

An American outfit, Page Communications Engineers, has offices in our apartment building and in the building next door. They got a direct hit in the shelling of November 1. We heard that just today eight of their people up in Dalat were killed in an explosion, presumably set off by the VC. I will certainly breathe easier when I get away from this country. As it stands now, I'm scheduled to be in Bangkok in less than 48 hours—as you see I'm counting the hours now.

November 26, 1966

Dearest Jackie,

Since I should be long gone from Saigon by the time you read this, I'll admit things have not been very reassuring even in the city itself. Every day's paper carries some note of bombs or grenades going off right in the city, and generally directed at Americans. A favorite stunt is to catch the Americans where they gather in the morning rush hour to wait for buses or cars. The general rule on Americans congregating on the streets is: Two's company, three's a crowd.

Most of the Vietnamese people are poor and have very little, but they do seem to have most of what they need. Their own leaders seem to have just about as little kindness for them as the VC does. So I often think — if we lost this war, a few big shots would suffer but the majority of the people wouldn't care and would be at least as well off as they are now. Mostly, they need to be left alone to make their living. The only way I can justify the American involvement in my own mind is as an act of pure power politics to define our image to all Asians, an act in which the destiny of the South Vietnamese just happens to be involved.

So small wonder that South Vietnamese soldiers fight less enthusiastically than the Americans do.

November 27, 1966

Dearest Jackie,

Yesterday's flight from Saigon to Bangkok was two hours late, The contrast of the two cities is extreme. After so many years of war, Saigon is pretty much a hovel, whereas Bangkok — what I have seen of it — is full of modern buildings and fine boulevards. Our hotel is new, air-conditioned, and has elevators you don't have to wait ten-deep in line for.

A Thai driver picked me up at 7 AM for a tour. It was called the "floating market" tour, by boat. About 2½ hours in a motor launch, just the driver and I, for $5.00. Toured along the river and through a long canal that people live along just like a street. Made several stops: at a Buddhist temple, at a place where the royal barges are kept, and at the floating market where they sell many foods and all sorts of souvenir items, have a room full of silk looms, and have a pet elephant and monkeys.

For the first time in my recent travels, I felt the urge to do some shopping. I went through about $20, leaving barely enough Thai money to pay the boatman. We are lucky that they are having unusually cool weather here—normally Bangkok is hotter than Saigon, they say. But the morning air was actually refreshing, and I was wearing an undershirt!

IV. Parting Thoughts

My thoughts about the Vietnam War are not those of a political or historical expert. I am a career geologist who, through many years in the Civil Service, tended to avoid political involvements. My work brought me into contact with American military operations in several parts of the world, including Vietnam. I believe that the Vietnam experience carries powerful lessons concerning the unilateral initiation of wars by our political leaders. These lessons had not been learned by 2003 when the United States invaded Iraq. They deserve the raising of many voices, not just those of the experts.

* * *

Until 1966, like many middle-class Americans, I accepted the justification for the Vietnam War that our leaders gave us: a defense of South Vietnam against aggressive expansion and control by the major communist powers. That threat seemed to be supported by the words of Nikita Khrushchev, Premier of the Soviet Union, when he hailed the development of such "Wars of National Liberation" as the new model for spreading communist doctrine and control, and for overcoming resistance by the capitalistic nations.

This justification seemed to make sense. Through the decade following World War II, the devastated countries of Eastern Europe had fallen one by one under Soviet control, enforced where necessary by troops and tanks. China had replaced its former government, our wartime ally, with a communist dictatorship. When forces from North Korea invaded South Korea, we rose to its defense. A victory there seemed within our grasp until Chinese forces entered the fray, ultimately producing a stalemate that persists to this day. No wonder, then, that Mr. Khrushchev sought a newer, fresher model for expansion.

I assumed that the people of South Vietnam wanted, needed, and deserved defense against communist aggression. Without defense, they would succumb to it as the North Vietnamese had already done.

Dissenters held that the major goal of the Vietnamese people, north and south, was national independence following many years of occupation and colonial status. Communism was a distant secondary issue. I was mindful of these issues while in Vietnam, but could not make any personal resolution of them.

Nevertheless, two letters from Vietnam indicated a first significant shift in attitude:

November 22, 1966

"The people here seem to be happy with very little. The lame (very few of these in evidence), the wounded, and those who are caught in the battlefields are the ones I feel most sorry for. But the general picture is one of "life as normal," with Americans seeming to take the war much more seriously than the Vietnamese. I suspect that most of the Vietnamese would just like to be left alone."

November 26, 1966

"Most of the Vietnamese people are poor and have very little, but they do seem to have most of what they need. Their own leaders seem to have just about as little kindness for them as the VC does. So I often think — if we lost this war, a few big shots would suffer but the majority of the people wouldn't care and would be at least as well off as they are now. Mostly, they need to be left alone to make their living. The only way I can justify the American involvement in my own mind is as an act of pure power politics to define our image to all Asians, an act in which the destiny of the South Vietnamese just happens to be involved.

"So, small wonder that South Vietnamese soldiers fight less enthusiastically than the Americans do."

By "pure power politics" I was referring to America's need to demonstrate that we would react strongly to Mr. Khrushchev's new model, the "Wars of National Liberation." This seemed to be valid in the competition between America and the Soviet Union, but it was different and less "noble" than defending the Vietnamese people. They might well be the victims instead.

* * *

**Like many Americans, I had a further shift of attitude in
1968, triggered by two events early in the year: the Battle of Khe
Sanh and the Tet Offensive.**

The Khe Sanh operation, 21 January to 9 July 1968, was ba-
sically a siege operation against a major American combat base
by an estimated force of 20,000 troops of the National Liberation
Front and the North Vietnamese army. The Americans dropped over
100,000 tons of bombs (five times the explosive power of the atomic
bomb at Hiroshima), and they conducted an overland relief expedi-
tion that finally broke the siege. However, they chose to dismantle
the base rather than risk similar battles in the future. It was the first
time in Vietnam that we abandoned a major base because of enemy
pressure.

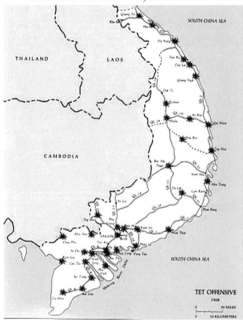

The Tet Offensive, launched on 30 January 1968, quickly became a well coordinated,
countrywide attack by
more than 80,000 com-
munist troops against
more than 100 towns and
cities. The accompany-
ing map shows some of
their targets. Though this
offensive was eventually
defeated, Americans were
shocked. They had been
assured that previous de-
feats had rendered the
communist forces inca-
pable of launching such a
massive effort.

This was more than a major failure of intelligence. It was also a failure to track the progress of the war in any realistic sense. Our military and political leaders were charged with many things, ranging from malfeasance to stupidity.

The charge that I chose was incompetence, not of persons but of institutions at the highest levels of military management. My experience at the Research Analysis Corporation (RAC), now approaching two years, had opened my eyes to entirely new techniques for planning and executing war, and for tracking its progress. The buzzwords of the time were Systems Analysis, Systems Management, and Operations Research. RAC had a front seat in this development, having originated as the Operations Research Office of Johns Hopkins University. I came to believe that these techniques had much to do with the incompetence I observed.

Secretary of Defense Robert S. McNamara had successfully developed and used the techniques during his tenure as one of the "Whiz Kids" at Ford Motor Company, and later as the firm's president. He promoted their widespread adoption at the Pentagon. They were highly quantitative, meaning that factors could not be considered unless they could be counted, measured, or weighed. Other factors, judgmental, had to be put aside regardless of their importance.

One example of this was in a poster on the wall of the RAC field office in Saigon: It tracked progress in the program to win the hearts and minds of people in the villages. The counts of villages won increased steadily over time, seeming to indicate that victory was just around the corner. I never understood how they could deal quantitatively with such matters. Maybe they conducted opinion polls.

As a second example, a RAC analyst lectured us on how he tracked the success of a siege against a VC stronghold in the Iron Triangle. His technique was to calculate a ratio between quantities of ammunition fired into the stronghold, versus the quantities fired back at our troops. While the American firing maintained a steady high level, return fire from the VC dwindled until it became only a trickle of sniper fire. This seemed to indicate an American victory. Shortly afterward, however, prisoner-of–war interrogations revealed that the VC had not been defeated. Understandably, their troops had merely moved back to get out of the range of our guns.

Both of these examples show the types of error that led to the twin shocks of Khe Sanh and Tet.

I based my shift of attitude on the following observations:

During this reign of incompetence, we were conducting brute-force tactics, such as the bombing at Khe Sanh and the destruction of tunnels by B-52 carpet bombing. The numbers of deaths and the extent of environmental destruction were simply not justified by goals that we were unlikely to reach in any event.

Another factor: Still impressed by the magnificent, brave American soldiers I had seen in 1966, I was troubled now by reports of disillusioned soldiers and "potheads." Were we degrading our military forces through this ill-advised campaign?

And finally: American unity was seriously threatened by controversy at home. The year 1968 saw particularly violent demonstrations in the streets. Splits were developing between social and ethnic groups, and between generations.

I now believed that, regardless of any remaining justification for the war, we needed to get out of Vietnam, the sooner the better.

I still clung to one thin thread of possible justification: The war might be a necessary strategy in our competition with the major communist powers.

* * *

Finally, in the very early 1970s, I began to question that one remaining thread. I attended lectures by a number of statesmen and other leaders for whom I had respect. The most memorable was probably Edward Teller, dubbed Father of the Hydrogen Bomb. I had come to expect that he would be hawkish (supportive of war) in his politics. Unanimously with all the others, he insisted that the American performance in Vietnam, from the Kennedy through the Nixon administrations, was driven solely by "domestic political considerations."

To me this meant: Not for defense of the Vietnamese people, not for a necessary strategy in our competition with the Sino-Soviet bloc. Merely a means of getting out the vote.

I then began digging into the histories of Ho Chi Minh; of America's relationships with various successive governments in the Republic of Vietnam; and of Vietnam's conduct since the war – the conduct of an independent nation rather than a communist satellite. The details are readily available. Here I will only summarize that Ho Chi Minh comes through primarily as a nationalist, and only secondarily as a man of communist leanings. In fact, when seeking freedom from France, he turned first to the U.S. for aid, only later to the communist powers.

By the end of this process, I had lost every shred of belief that this war was justified.

One cannot overstress the importance of the lessons to be learned from this experience. When George W. Bush ordered the invasion of Iraq in 2003, justified mainly by a network of misinformation and outright lies, it was clear that we had not yet learned.

66011458R00040

Made in the USA
Middletown, DE
07 March 2018